W9-ANR-539

Geography Starts

RIVERS

Andy Owen
and
Miranda Ashwell

Heinemann Interactive Library
Des Plaines, Illinois

© 1998 Reed Educational & Professional Publishing
Published by Heinemann Interactive Library,
an imprint of Reed Educational & Professional Publishing,
Chicago, IL

Customer Service 888-454-2279

Visit our website at www.heinemannlibrary.com

Designed by Susan Clarke

Illustrations by Oxford Illustrators (maps pp.23, 25, 27)
Printed in China by WKT Company Limited

06
10 9 8 7 6 5 4

Library of Congress Cataloging-in-Publication Data
Owen, Andy, 1961-
    Rivers / Andy Owen and Miranda Ashwell.
        p.   cm. — (Geography starts)
    Includes bibliographical references and index.
    Summary: An introduction to the types and characteristics of
rivers and to their formation, drainage, and floods.
    ISBN 1-57572-609-2 (lib. bdg.)   ISBN 1-58810-977-1 (pbk. bdg.)
    1. Rivers—Juvenile literature. [1. Rivers.] I. Ashwell,
Miranda, 1957- . II. Title. III. Series: Owen, Andy, 1961-
Geography starts.
GB1203.8.094   1998
551.48'3—dc21
                                                                    97-34419
                                                                       CIP
                                                                       AC

Acknowledgments
The publishers would like to thank the following for permission to reproduce photographs:
Aerofilms, p. 14; Air Fotos Ltd, p. 15; Andy Owen, pp. 7, 9; Colourific/Thomas Muscionico, p. 12; Environmental
Images/Graham Burns, p. 19; Images Colour Library, p. 10; Magnum/S.T. Franklin, p. 13; NRSC, pp. 22, 24, 26; Oxford
Scientific Films, p. 17 (Paul McCullagh), p. 20 (Edward Parker); Panos Pictures/Neil Cooper, p. 28; Planet Earth/Adam
Jones, p. 21; Still Pictures, p. 29 (Andre Bartschi), p. 16 (Helour Netocny), p. 8 (Jim Wark); Telegraph Colour
Library/Terry McCormick, p. 11; Tony Stone, p. 5, p. 18 (Mark Lewis); Wildlife Matters, pp. 4, 6

Cover photograph: Robert Harding Picture Library / Nigel Francis

Our thanks to Betty Root for her comments in the preparation of this book.

Every effort has been made to contact copyright holders of any material reproduced in this book. Any omissions will
be rectified in subsequent printings if notice is given to the publisher.

Some words are shown in bold, **like this**. You can find
out what they mean by looking in the glossary.

Contents

Where Rivers Begin 4

Mountain Rivers 6

Bends in the River 8

Waterfalls 10

Floods 12

Rivers Meet the Sea 14

Getting River Water 16

Dirty Rivers 18

Work on the River 20

River Map 1 22

River Map 2 24

River Map 3 26

Amazing River Facts 28

Glossary 30

More Books to Read 31

Index 32

Where Rivers Begin

A river is a large body of water that **flows** over land. The start of a river is called the source.

This river begins in the mountains where there is a lot of rain and snow.

This river flows fast as it runs down the mountain.

Some rivers start when ice melts. The ice melts in warm weather. The river is the deepest in spring and summer.

Mountain Rivers

two streams join to make a river

Water **flows** down the hill in a stream.
It grows into a bigger river as other
streams join it.

Water tumbles over rocks as it flows down hill. Over many years, stones in the stream become round and smooth.

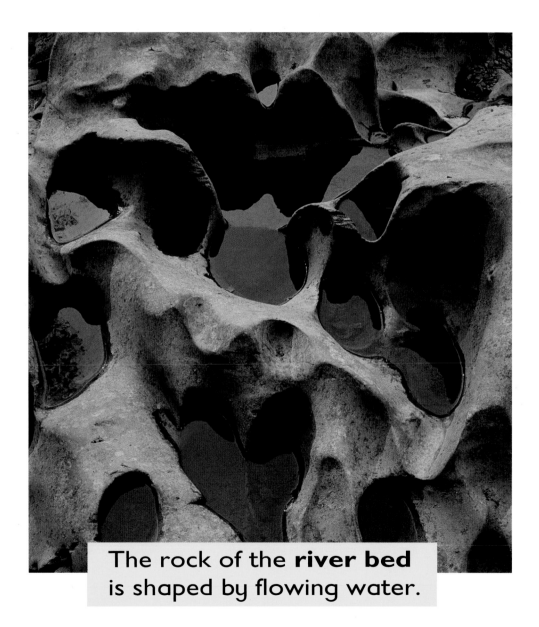

The rock of the **river bed** is shaped by flowing water.

Bends in the River

On flat land, the river makes large bends, or curves. These bends are called meanders.

The **flowing** water has made these bends.

Water flows quickly around the bend.
It washes away the **river bank** and
makes a cliff.

This bank was made by
the meander in the river.

Waterfalls

Where a river drops over a steep cliff it makes a waterfall. The rock below is worn away by the falling water.

The falling water makes lots of spray.

This raft is tossed about by the wild water.

The river is wild and rough below the waterfall. The river **flows** very fast over large rocks. This part of the river is called the **rapids**.

Floods

Heavy rain fills the river. Sometimes water spills over and floods the land. The flat land next to the river is called the flood plain.

Some rivers flood every year.

Flood water drops mud
onto the farmland.

When rivers flood they carry mud onto
the land. This mud helps plants grow well.
Flood plains make good farmland.

Rivers Meet the Sea

Rivers are often very wide where they meet the sea. This is called the river mouth. The river then flows into the sea.

This river mouth is very wide.

Large factories have been built on the flat land near the river mouth.

The river drops mud at the river mouth. The mud makes flat land next to the river. This land is called mud flats.

Getting River Water

Water is taken from rivers to use on the land. This farmer is lifting water to put on his fields.

lifting water by hand

This farmer is using a pump to lift water.
The pump works very quickly so the
farmer has lots of water.

lifting water with a machine

Dirty Rivers

Garbage from homes and factories gets into the river. It makes the water dirty. This is called **pollution**.

You should not drink polluted water.

Fish will live in the river
when it is clean.

Dirty water kills fish and river plants.
People clean the river to make it safe.

Work on the River

People use rivers in many ways.
Fish from the river are sold for food.

This man catches fish with a net.

Boats carry people and things on the river. Some rivers are made deeper and wider for big ships and **barges** to use.

This large barge is carrying **coal.**

River Map 1

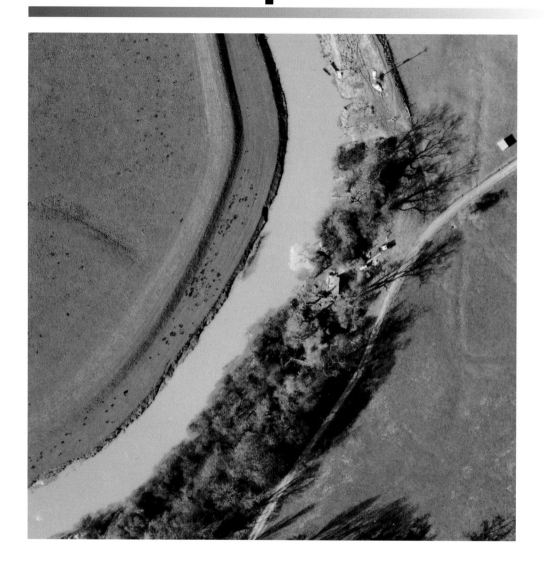

This photo was taken from an airplane. You can see a large bend in the river. There are fields and woods next to the river.

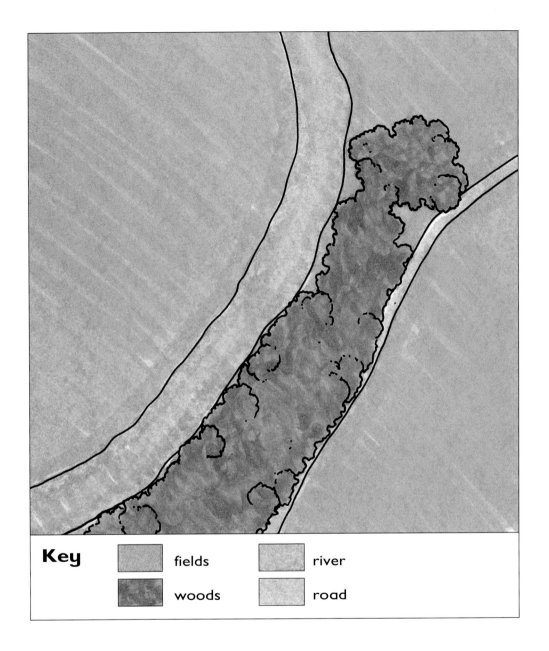

Key

	fields		river
	woods		road

Maps are pictures of the land.
This map shows us the same place
as the photo.

River Map 2

This is a photo of the same river. The bend looks smaller, but you can see more of the river. You can also see a farm.

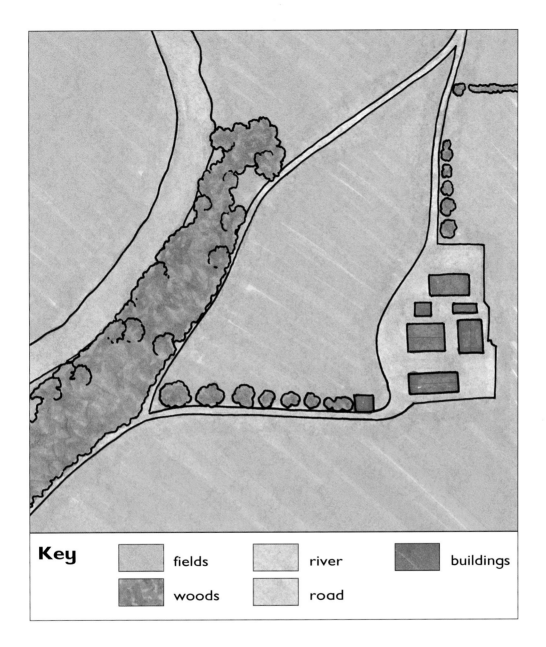

Key

fields	river	buildings
woods	road	

You can understand the map by using the key. The blue line shows the river and the gray line shows the road to the farm.

River Map 3

In this photo, you can see more of the river and more fields. There is a bridge crossing the river at the top of the photo.

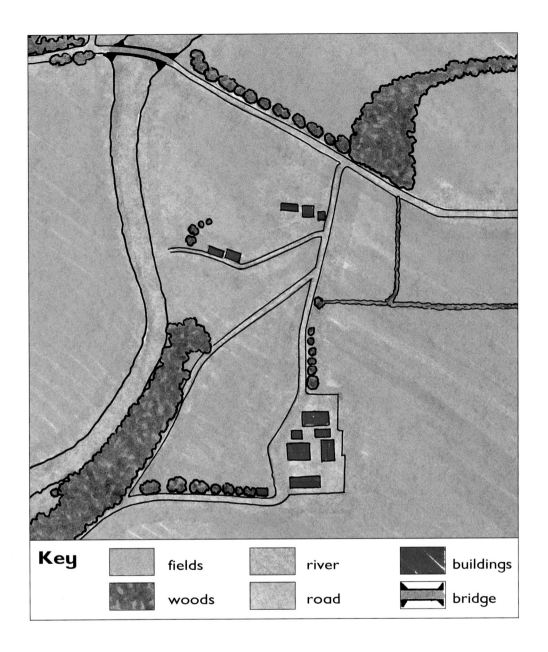

Key

fields	river	buildings
woods	road	bridge

The green on the map shows the fields.
You can see the shape of each field.

Amazing River Facts

The Amazon River in South America has more water than any other river in the world. It also **flows** through the biggest rainforest in the world.

The Nile River is the longest river in the world. Most of the river flows through a huge desert.

The Nile river is 4,145 miles (6,673 kilometers) long.

Glossary

barges large flat-bottom boats

coal brown or black rock that gives off heat when burned

flows movement of water

pollution dirt and garbage in the water or air

rapids where a river flows fast over rocks

river bank sides of a river

river bed the bottom of a river

More Books to Read

Baker, Susan. *First Look at Rivers.* Milwaukee: Gareth Stevens, 1991.

Carlisle, Norman and Madelyn. *Rivers.* Danbury, Conn: Children's Press, 1982.

Cherry, Lynn. *A River Ran Wild: An Environmental History.* New York: Harcourt Brace, 1992.

Crump, Donald J. ed. *Let's Explore a River.* Washington, D.C.: National Geographic, 1988.

Fowler, Allen. *All Along the River.* Danbury, Conn: Childrens Press, 1994.

Theodorou, Rod and Carole Telford. *Amazing Journeys: Down a River.* Des Plaines, Ill: Heinemann Interactive Library, 1997.

Index

flood plain 12, 13

floods 12, 13

maps 23, 25, 27

meanders 8, 9

mouth 14, 15

mud flats 15

pollution 18, 19

rapids 11

river bank 9

river bed 7

river uses 16, 17, 20, 21

source 4

stream 6, 7

waterfalls 10, 11